The Wonderful Man

for Wonderful Men everywhere

☆

ISBN-13: 978-0-7407-7808-7
ISBN-10: 0-7407-7808-0

09 10 11 12 13 SDB 10 9 8 7 6 5 4 3 2 1

www.edwardmonkton.com

www.andrewsmcmeel.com

ATTENTION: SCHOOLS AND BUSINESSES

Andrews McMeel books are available at quantity discounts with bulk purchase for educational, business, or sales promotional use. For information, please write to: Special Sales Department, Andrews McMeel Publishing, LLC, 1130 Walnut Street, Kansas City, Missouri 64106.

THE WONDERFUL MAN

Edward Monkton

**Andrews McMeel
Publishing, LLC**

Kansas City

Once upon a time there was a MAN.

And the WONDERFUL thing about this man was that...

...he was ORDINARY.

He did not have a
great SINGING voice
and a FASHIONABLE
hairstyle.

He did not have
ENORMOUS muscles
and a "WINNING"
smile.

He did not have a big LIMOUSINE and a ladyfriend with overly large BREASTS and overly tight outfits.

(Let us call these people The "Impressive" People for now.)

But there was one thing this man DID have and it was a thing of great AMAZINGNESS.

This man was...

...NICE

And because he was NICE, and because he went about his ORDINARY business in his own QUIET way, he had a STRANGE and alarming effect on people.

"Hello!" he said to the man with the great SINGING voice and FASHIONABLE hairstyle.

"WEIRDO!" said the man.

"NICE DAY!" he said to the man with ENORMOUS MUSCLES and a "WINNING" smile.

"What do you WANT?" said the man.

"You've dropped your cigars," he said to the man with the big LIMOUSINE and the ladyfriend with overly large BREASTS and overly tight outfits.

"Go away!" said the man.

But with his pleasant manner, his kind words and his cheery nature, small WISPS of NICENESS blew from The ORDINARY Man like seeds in the wind and they PLANTED themselves deep into the HEARTS of The "Impressive" People.

These seeds began to GROW and it wasn't long before The "Impressive" People felt twinges of NICENESS, small urges of PLEASANTNESS and twinklings of GENEROSITY.

And they liked it.

"Impressive" People being what they are, word of The Ordinary Man soon spread. Some called him a GURU and some a great HEALER.

And they gave him a name which was The WONDERFUL Man.

And one by one, all the people peeled off their skins of WEALTH, of POWER, of FEAR, of ANGER and of GREED, and they began to wallow and swim NAKED TOGETHER in the soft warm waters of LOVELINESS.

THE END